50 Ways To Motivate Yourself In 50 Minutes

Discover 50 Motivational Hacks To Build Self-Discipline, Achieve Your Goals And Get What You Want

Table of Contents

Introduction

I want to thank you and congratulate you for downloading the book, *50 Ways To Motivate Yourself In 50 Minutes: Discover 50 Motivational Hacks To Build Self-Discipline, Achieve Your Goals And Get What You Want.*

This book contains proven steps and strategies on how to be able to motivate yourself no matter what your circumstances are. If you find that you just can't bring yourself to go through the necessary actions, then you more than likely lack the motivation. Motivation is something that isn't simply found. You have to make it happen!

You've fallen into a rut. All you want to do when you get home is sit on the couch and watch television. Meanwhile, dishes are building up in the sink and the laundry needs to be done. You look at all this and simply push it aside until later. However, what happens when you don't feel like doing it later? In this book, I'm going to provide you with some practical ways to drive yourself to do what needs to be done and go much further. So, if you have a motivation problem, look no further!

Thanks again for downloading this book, I hope you enjoy it!

Chapter 1- Motivating Yourself in the Morning

I don't know about you, but the mornings are the least favorite part of my day. I'm not a morning person and never have been. Getting up and going are both a struggle to me. A real struggle. I find that I'm less productive and in a bad mood early in the mornings. One day, I knew that this cycle needed to change. Why should the mornings be any different than the rest of the day? I should start out energetic, driven and motivated in the morning and maintain that healthy attitude throughout the day.

After making that decision, I tried to think of ways that I could motivate myself early in the mornings so that I could have a successful and motivated day. During my journey, I have come up with a few hacks that have helped me start my day off with a boost of motivation and keep it going for the remainder of the day

Messages on the Mirror

If you're like a lot of people, you tend to look at yourself in the mirror first thing in the morning. You either note how horrible you look or you already have a plan for how you're going to shape your look for the rest of the day. I tend to find myself astounded by the person I see staring back. How can I have a good day with that person? So, the first hack I tried out to alleviate this problem was to write self-affirming messages on my mirror and change them periodically. I used a dry erase marker, and I looked at it whenever I looked at the mirror.

Find a message that will inspire you to be your best, even if you don't look or feel it. This will help build your self-image and make you start your day out on a positive note.

Positive Self Talk

Some mornings, the first thought that goes through my head when the alarm clock goes off is "yeah, right..." I have no motivation to get out of bed, and I'm already mentally dooming myself to a bummer of a day. So, to solve this problem, I began to tell myself something positive that would help me start the day off right. For example, I would tell myself that "I can do this!" By affirming myself in this way, it made it easier for me to get out of bed and get going in the mornings.

A Boost of Energy

Everything is good in moderation. I find that my boost of energy comes from a cup of coffee. It's a beverage I enjoy and it gives me that chemical boost of energy that I need in order to get a jump start on the day. However, if you find that you're dependent on caffeine to keep you going during the day, you need to evaluate a healthier approach to finding energy during the day.

Stay on a Regular Schedule

I'm always more motivated when I know what to expect. So, I made it a point to know my schedule and stick to my personal schedule as much as I possibly could. Things do happen that can interrupt a schedule, but knowing that I have one planned and in place makes it much easier to keep on track and still stay productive during the day.

Don't Hit Snooze

"Just five more minutes…" That is one phrase that can zap your motivation quickly. By hitting your snooze button and making it a habit, you're basically procrastinating the inevitable task of getting up and going. I find that I lack motivation when I hit that snooze button. Five minutes of snooze time isn't going to do you many favors, so don't get in the habit of using it.

Breakfast is Key

Having a healthy and balanced breakfast is the key to starting out your day right. Food is energy, so eating in the morning and eating the right types of foods will help you to stay focused on whatever you're pursuing during the day. Even if you feel pressed for time, have a go to meal that will provide you with the nutrition you need in order to start the day out right.

Have a Routine

Having a routine every morning sounds boring, but it can help you gain motivation to boost you into your day. Knowing what to expect and knowing that once it's done what comes next will help propel your day. I find that a change in my routine actually makes it difficult for me to think clearly and have a productive day. However, doing the same general activities in the same order helps me to get going.

Make Waking Up a Game

This is a fun way to get my day going. When I first wake up, I try to guess what will happen first when I arrive at work or what I will see first on television when I flip it on. By making the uncertainties of the day a guessing game, I stay focused on what is going to happen next rather than just floating through the day.

Morning Exercise

I find that taking a morning walk or having a morning trip to the gym is extremely motivating. It helps get my heart pumping and gets me moving so that I don't feel sleepy or lethargic. Even if you just stretch when you wake up, it will help increase your blood flow and help you get moving.

Even if you're not a morning person, these are some ways that you can get yourself moving in the morning and help you get a jump start on the day. I find that if I start out with a good attitude, it tends to last throughout the day. So, make your mornings the start of your motivation!

Chapter 2- Motivating Yourself When You Don't Have Much Energy

We all face those moments when energy and motivation are totally nonexistent. You might even doubt how you're going to make it through the day. Caffeine might be your go to and after the rush fades away, you crash. These days can be difficult, but they don't have to be impossible to get through. By trying different methods to energize and motivate yourself, you can be on your way to having a productive day even if you don't have too much energy to begin with.

Supplements

Taking energy supplements can definitely boost your productivity and willingness to achieve what you have planned. Try using herbs such as ginseng and vitamin B12 to help you get a good boost of energy that will propel you into the rest of your day. Also, make sure that you take a multivitamin on a daily basis, as this will help boost your energy levels and drive to get going.

One Step at a Time

Concentrate on one action at a time. If you think about everything that you have to do, then your energy levels will feel even lower. Take your routine one action at a time and don't focus on what you have left to do. This might seem like a slow way to go, but if you're only focused on the immediate action, then you won't mentally deplete the energy you have left.

Keep at it

Get moving and keep moving. Energy isn't some magic thing that lives in a bottle and can be taken on a whim. Sometimes you have to force yourself to go and keep going. I find that once I get going and maintain momentum that I will be more likely to continue being productive and finishing what I started out to accomplish in the first place. Don't fool yourself by telling yourself that you'll be able to do it later. That is only procrastinating and will ultimately put a lot of unwanted tasks on the back burner.

Have Someone to Pep Talk You

For a while, I had absolutely no motivation or energy for anything. I got the point where I just gave up. When a good friend noticed my attitude, he began to encourage me and give me pep talks in order to help me achieve what I set out to do. By having an outside source encouraging me, I found that I believed in myself even more and a few motivational words helped boost my drive. Even if I call someone for a quick pep talk, this is still a quick way for me to get up and going when I have no energy at all.

Think of Things that Energize You

When I lack energy, thinking of things that motivate and energize me give me that necessary boost to get going. It can be something like my children or the award that I received for my work performance. Whatever the thought that will motivate me, I will play that thought over in my head as I pursue the not so pleasant tasks that I might face when I'm less than motivated and lack energy.

Listen to Upbeat Music

I find that music can really dictate my moods. When I'm melancholy, listening to sad music will fuel that mood. So, why not use music to set a motivational mood in place? Upbeat and positive music really help me to get going when I feel less than enthusiastic. I now have a playlist on my MP3 player that has music just for the purpose of energizing me when I feel lethargic. Try finding some upbeat tunes that you like to listen to and play them when you lack energy and see if they won't have a positive effect on your energy level!

Rewarding Yourself When You Accomplish a Difficult Task

If I find that I'm faced with a difficult situation or task, I will set up a reward for myself when I complete it successfully. Once, I was moving by myself and needed to get the job done in a specific amount of time. However, I felt less than motivated to get the task done at all. So, I told myself that once I got everything moved and unpacked, I would go and buy myself something that I had wanted for a while. This motivated me to keep going with the task and accomplish it in the time frame that I wanted to get it done in. As I walked out of the store with my new toy, I felt accomplished and motivated to continue in my positive behavior.

Have Others Spur You On

Other people can be a great resource when it comes to motivation. I found this especially true when I was trying to start my career. The classes that I was taking were difficult and I felt as though I wanted to give up. However, I found some supportive friends and family who through tough love helped me to achieve my overall goal and get to where I am today. By using others as a resource for motivation, I had an outside source that kicked me in the behind when I slacked or was about ready to give up altogether. I recommend that if you have a supportive group of people in your life, or even just one supportive person, use them as a source of motivation so that you won't give up when it gets tough.

Being motivated when you lack energy can be very difficult. While you don't want to rely on chemicals to get you going, sometimes you feel as if that is your only resort. However, don't fool yourself into thinking that is the only way to gain motivation and energy! Try different ways to perk up and get going! I have only provided a few ideas. Think of some that might help you in your own personal circumstances and try them when you're feeling tired and not so energetic!

Chapter 3- Motivational Hacks When You Feel Overwhelmed

When life gets overwhelming, many tend to find that their emotional response is to shut down. I know that when I'm feeling like there is too much going on in my world, I want to run away from it rather than keep going and pursuing the final result. However, nothing gets accomplished if you shut down. Finding ways to stay motivated even if you're feeling like it's too much to handle will help you to make it through life's toughest circumstances. In this chapter, I'm going to give you some suggestions on how to keep yourself motivated when life feels like it's piling everything on you at once.

Leave Yourself Notes

I find that if I leave myself little encouraging notes in places that I look often that I feel better. One of my favorite things to do is to use the sticky note feature on the desktop of my computer and write some encouraging notes to myself. When I get on the computer, I see them and am reminded that I can do this and make it through whatever challenges that life throws my direction.

Track Your Progress

When the pile of to dos seems longer than what you have done, take a moment and think of all the things you have accomplished during a certain period of time. By saying to yourself that you might not be where you wanted to be at that moment, at least you got this thing done and that it was a big chore on your long to do list. Giving yourself that small pat on the back will keep you motivated and help you to continue with whatever tasks you still need to perform.

Make Small Goals

It's easy to get overwhelmed when you set your standards and your goals too high. I find that if I set small and attainable goals from the beginning, I stay motivated when I reach them and am ready to move on to the next step. If I set my goals and standards too high to begin with, it's easy to get discouraged and feel overwhelmed when I don't make the progress that I wanted to make when I originally set the goal.

Take One Project at a Time

Multitasking always seems like a good idea until you find yourself in the middle of a half dozen unfinished projects. Not only do you still have to complete each project, but it feels like you cannot even complete one. So, I found that if I put my complete effort towards one project at a time and see it through to the end before I begin the next one, I feel more productive and feel like I have achieved what I set out to do. I also feel less overwhelmed because I'm not stuck in the middle of too many projects at the same time.

Turn Away for a Moment

When I find that I'm incredibly overwhelmed by a task, I sometimes turn away from that particular task or project for a moment or even a few hours until I can think more clearly. If I keep on trying at something that has me frustrated and overwhelmed, then don't get much further and only become more agitated. It's not wrong to step away from something and come back to it once you have a clearer perspective.

Sing a Song

I like silly songs. When I feel especially stressed out and overwhelmed, I will sing a silly song to myself that will lift my spirits. Being in a better mood, I find that I have a more positive outlook for the project and I feel more motivated to finish it and finish it well. It doesn't even have to be a silly song. I have found a few inspirational songs that have helped motivate me when I'm at my wits end.

Clear Your Mind

When you feel totally overwhelmed, step away from the circumstance or project and take a deep breath. Allow your mind to relax and clear itself from the stress that it might be experiencing at that moment. Going into something with a clear mind will give you a fresh and refreshing perspective that will help you stay motivated and productive.

We all have moments in our lives where we lack motivation when we feel stressed and overwhelmed. Everyone has different stressors, so knowing what stresses you out and how to alleviate that stress are good ways to stop yourself from feeling overwhelmed. Find ways that you can keep yourself going even when you're beginning to feel overwhelmed by life.

Just because you feel stressed out doesn't mean that the world is going to stop until you don't feel that way. Take charge of your drive and motivation and make it happen!

Chapter 4- Hacks to Build Self-Discipline

People who are more self-disciplined tend to be more successful at whatever they put their minds to. It's tough to keep yourself in line sometimes. Everyone has their temptations and vices that will make them stray from their ultimate goals. However, being disciplined will help you define your limits and know when you're getting out of line with your goals and expectations. So, when you find that you have no self-discipline, try to find ways to build that discipline and keep it strong whenever you see an opportunity to stray.

Plan a Routine

Having a plan and sticking to a plan is a great method for keeping yourself disciplined. Personally, I get distracted easily, and that is one of the quickest ways that I can go off course. However, by taking time to have a set routine and sticking to it on a regular basis, I find that I keep myself in line and keep myself motivated throughout the day. It takes some time to get a productive routine down, but once you have it, it's a quick way to ensure that you are disciplined and staying motivated throughout the day.

Keep to Your Routine as Closely as Possible

Life has a funny way of interrupting our best laid plans. However, it's how we handle life's distractions that will make us successful. So, when you find that something is interrupting your routine, get past it as soon as possible and carry on with your routine as if it didn't happen. By sticking by your routine, you will be more likely to keep the momentum of your day going in high gear.

Have the Same Routine Daily

It can get incredibly confusing if you change your routine too often. Have one routine and work towards keeping it consistent from day to day. A routine can help you continue a consistent flow throughout your day. It might take a little bit to get your routine into place, but once you do, you will be well on your way to having a driving force that will propel you through the day.

Have Specific Goals

Goals are an important part of motivation. If you don't know what you're aiming for, then you basically walking in circles. So, have specific goals for whatever you would like to achieve in place before you go for it. By knowing what you want and what you expect to gain from the activity will make you more motivated to give it your complete and total effort.

Design Your Life to Fit Around Your Goals

Knowing what you want to accomplish is a good factor to motivate you to succeed in achieving it. So, once you know what you want and what your goals are for the outcome, structure your activities around the goal. This can be simply telling yourself that you want to be at this place at this specific time.

Have a Goal Pinup Board

I have a cork board in my kitchen that I will pin my goals up on. By looking at them on a regular basis, I find that it rekindles my motivation to continue with pursuing them. This is a quick and inexpensive way to visually motivate yourself. I have also found that if a person or a pet motivates me to do a certain task, I will hang their pictures up where they can motivate me to continue on.

Organize Your Day

Taking a few moments to organize my day helps me to stay productive and motivated during the day. Nothing is more discouraging than finding that something isn't where I planned for it to be and I'm going to have to spend a lot of time finding it. By taking a few moments to plan ahead and organize how I want to spend my day, I find that it keeps me on track and where I would like to be at the end of the day.

Self-discipline can be a difficult area to cultivate. We are our toughest critics, but we are also the first ones to throw in the towel when life gets tough. By taking a few moments to but these hacks into practice, you can keep yourself on track and stay productive and motivated no matter what the circumstances might be.

Chapter 5- Hacks for Getting Yourself Going

Getting myself going is often the most difficult part of my day. If I'm feeling less than motivated, this can be a difficult and frustrating challenge. However, it's not impossible to get yourself motivated and productive even if you're not feeling like you're ready to go. By taking a few moments and putting a few of these hacks into practice, you will begin to feel your spirits rise along with your motivation!

Have a Theme Song

Yes, I admit, I have my own theme song. It is loosely based upon a cartoon theme song with my name entered into it, but it is a great motivator when I feel like I just want to sit there and let life beat me up. I just sing that song to myself and I feel like a super human all over again!!!

Talk Through Your Motions

If I talk through what I'm doing, I tend to pay more attention to what I'm doing. This saves me from wandering around aimlessly and forgetting what I wanted to do in the first place. So, tell yourself what you're doing as you're doing it. If you're around others, do this silently. When I'm aware of what I'm doing, then I tend to make my movements count more.

Praise Yourself for Small Victories

When I feel totally lethargic and not wanting to get moving, I will praise myself for the small things that I have accomplished. "Yay! I just combed my hair! That's one step closer to getting going than before!" It might seem silly, but it can be a great motivator, especially when you're lacking the drive and determination to get through the day.

Have a Personal Competition

I'm a very competitive person, so I found that if I give myself competitions, it helps me to get going faster. For example, I will sometimes tell myself that I got dressed much faster the day before and had more free time as result. This makes me want to step up my game at that moment so that I can do better than I did the day before. There are many different ways that you can have a personal competition. Just make it a way to better yourself and your motivational goals.

Challenge Yourself

Along with competition, I do enjoy a good challenge. So, I will motivate myself by challenging myself with new tasks daily. This keeps me excited to continue trying and also helps me to improve upon myself on my habits.

Allow Others to Challenge You

We've all seen movies where there is a competition between two of the characters as to who is going to be the best and win whatever the competition is. This competition fuels the desire to continue on in the journey. You want to be the best, and nothing is going to stop that from happening. If you have someone like that in your life, use them as a resource to help you find success and motivation. It doesn't' have to be a bloody battle, but a little competition can go a long ways in helping you to go further and accomplish more than you would under your own power.

Getting going when you lack motivation can be difficult. However, it doesn't take a lot of time to find small ways to motivate yourself and give yourself the boost you need in order to get through the day. Motivation is sometimes hard to come by, but if you can find ways to spark it, then you will be well on your way to staying motivated and self-disciplined. I find that others are my greatest resource for helping me to get and stay motivated. However, you might not have that resource, so finding something that will help spark that motivation is an important way to getting going and succeeding in what you're pursuing. Don't allow yourself to suffer because you simply cannot get motivated. Find ways to be motivated and strive to keep that fire going!

Chapter 6- Hacks for Creating Personal Success

Everyone wants to be successful. Whether it be at a job or at a specific task, we want to have something to show for our efforts. Whatever you want to pursue as your personal success, put your full efforts towards it and don't give up on it.

In this chapter, I'm going to suggest some hacks that will help you to boost your own personal success and help you to continue on to becoming an overall successful person.

Have a Plan

In order to be successful, you need to know what you want and how you plan to accomplish it. Be specific. What do you want, and what will it take for you to get to that point of achieving it? Ask yourself these questions. Know exactly what you're aiming for before you even begin. After you know what you want, then plan on how you're going to get there. For example, you have decided that you want to own your own home, but you don't have the necessary funds to put a down payment down on the type of home that you want. So, how will you be successful in your goal? Well, you decide that you're going to take on a second job in order to raise the money to make a decent down payment. Once you have that money, then you will continue your search for your own home. You know what you want and you have a plan to achieve that goal.

Know Your Opponents

No matter what you have planned, there will be people and other circumstance that will stand in your way. By knowing what these are, you stand a better chance at getting through these obstacles when the approach you. Going back to our example about purchasing a home, you find that your boss doesn't like you and cuts your hours so that you're not making much money. This is an opponent to your goal. Do whatever is necessary to sidestep this and continue toward your goal. It might be finding a different job or moving to a different area of the business. Find a good solution to get around this opponent.

Know Your Obstacles

Just like you will have opponents, you will also face unknown obstacles in your journey towards your goal. Your car breaks down and you have to invest in a new one, which takes some of the money you had saved for the down payment for your home. These are just minor setbacks that will make your goal seem further away. Recognize an obstacle when it arises and rise above it so it doesn't stop you from what you want to achieve.

Have a Driving Force

There is always something that is a force behind what we do. In the example of the house, the driving force might be the start of a family. You want a family badly, but you don't want to have one until you are stable and settled. Knowing what you want from the goal will help you to keep pursuing it, no matter how difficult it gets.

Stay Determined

If you lose your passion for what you're working towards, then you will lose the desire to keep on going. Stay determined and keep focused on the end goal. By having that focus and determination, you're allowing yourself the opportunity to succeed.

Don't Let Anyone Discourage You

There is always going to be someone out there who is going to mock and criticize your efforts. What you do with this treatment will ultimately determine your success. If you truly want what you're working towards, then don't let what anyone says discourage your efforts. What you ultimately let yourself believe can influence the final outcome of your goals and plans. Let yourself believe in your success and don't allow anyone else to stand in the way.

Fight for What You Want

Sometimes, you're going to be the only one who will be fighting for what you want. People might laugh and mock you for your efforts, but in the end, what you fight for is up to you. If you have a dream, don't let other people's opinions dictate how the outcome will look like. Be determined and motivated for what you want and not let anyone stand in your way.

Success is tough for some and it comes easily for others. Whatever success looks like for you, know what you want and what stands in your way to achievement. Be willing to go the extra mile and make the extra effort to succeed in whatever you set out to achieve.

Chapter 7- Building a More Motivated and Successful You

In the end, you are the one who controls whether or not you find success or failure. Sadly enough, many people set themselves back by having a negative self-image or outlook on their present situation. You might be one of those people who doesn't believe that you can ever be motivated or successful. Change that mindset! Every person on this earth is capable of achieving much more than they think! So, take some time and know what you want and what motivates you to achieve your goals.

You can be your best friend or your worst critic. It's ultimately up to you. So, the first decision that you must make is whether or not you're going to allow yourself to be set back or if you're not going to let anything stand in your way. Once you have made that decision, then you're ready to move on to the next phase. Hopefully, you chose not to let anything stand in your way. Let that be your mantra when times get rough. Just keep going....

Once you have a more positive and affirmative self-image, you will be ready to set goals and find success. Don't get me wrong, success can be difficult to achieve. However, your motivation and efforts make a world of difference when it comes to achieving the desired end result. Being a positive and encouraging resource to yourself is a key to ensuring your overall success. If you cannot find that positivity, find ways to find it. It might be friends, it might be a church group, or it might just come to you in a quiet moment. Once you find it, hold tight to it.

Success is something that everyone strives for their entire lives. However, many set themselves back by picking up bad habits and allowing themselves to limit their personal possibilities. Don't set yourself back in this way. If you find that you're a negative person, find ways to make your mindset positive. There is something out there for everyone. It might not be what you planned, but it will still be just right for you.

Motivation is the key to success. A lazy person doesn't accomplish anything. So, get up, take the reins and use the motivational hacks listed in this book to get yourself going. Put yourself out there in the world and make your dreams happen. In the end, you're the only influence on whether or not you lose or succeed. It's all in how you handle the challenges and the circumstances.

I hope that you have found the advice in this book useful to your pursuit of motivation and success. The tips that I have given are simple and can be completed in a small amount of time. Don't let time be an excuse for your failure. By using a few simple hacks, you can make a great difference in the way you use your time and build your motivation. I'm giving my ideas to you as a tool to help you to become a better you.

Take whatever is useful to you and use it to your advantage. I wish you all the luck and success that there is to be found in your life! You can do this! Don't let anything set you back!

Conclusion

Thank you again for downloading this book!

I hope this book was able to help you to quick and efficient ways to find motivation and build your success. Since motivation usually doesn't just appear, you have to figure out ways to motivate yourself and find the drive and desire to succeed. This book aims to help you to that in a quick and efficient way.

The next step is to try a few of the tips in this book to see if you can become more motivated and successful. It might be difficult at first to get yourself going, but once you do, you can be a force that will mean big changes for your life and those around you!

Finally, if you enjoyed this book, then I'd like to ask you for a favor, would you be kind enough to leave a review for this book on Amazon? It'd be greatly appreciated!

Click here to leave a review for this book on Amazon!

Made in the USA
Monee, IL
17 November 2022

17913528R00021